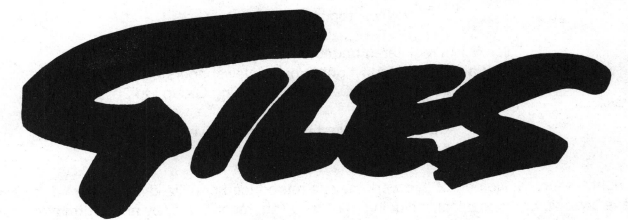

The Collection 2013

An Hachette UK Company
www.hachette.co.uk

First published in Great Britain in 2012 by Hamlyn,
a division of Octopus Publishing Group Ltd, Endeavour House, 189 Shaftesbury Avenue,
London, WC2H 8JY

www.octopusbooks.co.uk

Cartoons supplied by British Archive
Cartoons compiled by John Field

ISBN 13: 978-0-600-62455-4

A CIP catalogue record for this book is available
from the British Library.

Printed and bound in China

10 9 8 7 6 5 4 3 2 1

GILES

The Collection 2013

compiled by John Field

EXPRESS NEWSPAPERS

hamlyn

Contents

Foreword

Dick Strawbridge

I've never known a world without Giles cartoons – to me they epitomise Britishness. I'm particularly impressed by the thought of Giles sitting in front of a blank canvas and a short time later our world is précised in a picture and a couple of words. Having commented upon us for decades, it is even more remarkable that his observations are neither peevish nor cruel, in fact, it's hard not to love the family. Grandma has always been a little special to me, with her cold eyes, battle umbrella and resemblance to a Victorian Grim Reaper; she's formidable, but equally as endearing are the children, they take naughtiness to a new level and obviously belong to a pre-ASBO era.

Browsing through the books makes me smile on several levels, initially taking in the cartoon as a whole and then when I finally hoover up all the other quirky little snippets hidden in plain view. In the introduction to the very first annual of his cartoons, nearly sixty years ago, the Editor of the *Sunday Express* described Giles as "a spreader of happiness". His humour has proven timeless, but there is so much more to his work than just chuckles. Giles created evocative work that has spanned nearly all living memory. No doubt, I'm one of many who will look through this collection and thoroughly enjoy racking my brains trying to remember what was happening when they were drawn.

It's embarrassing to admit, but I rarely got my dose of Giles from the newspaper, it was always through the annuals and collections that seem to live in every family loo I've ever visited. Though that's not a bad thing, for where else can one find the time to dwell on Giles' work and fully appreciate the detail in every cartoon. Who knows, perhaps in 10 years I'll come across a well thumbed copy of this book in some privy library.

The Giles Family – Introduction

This year's Christmas collection presents a family album of one of Britain's most bewildering families. With several generations living together in the same house, family dynamics can often be fraught with misunderstandings and conflict and Giles's created family seems to encapsulate the chaos and turbulence of this multi-generational set-up.

The family made its first appearance in a cartoon dated August 5, 1945 just a few weeks after the end of WWII in Europe. Although this ending of hostilities in Europe brought a great deal of relief and joy, it also brought a major problem for Giles. His basic portfolio of subjects for his cartoons, the fighting forces, were, thankfully, no longer in action and his main villains, Hitler and co. were either dead or captured. This presented him with a major problem: where would he go to for good subjects for his humour in the future?

In his book, *The Giles Family*, Peter Tory recalls a conversation he had with Giles about the advent of the Giles family. Giles referred to the period just after the end of WWII:-

"All of my work for the Express up until then had been in the wartime. All the characters were wartime characters, or people caught up in the war. Suddenly they were gone. I had lost them – Hitler, Mussolini – disreputable little Franco was still there, of course – Himmler, Goering, Goebbels. I drew the family as something which could take their place. After that, whenever I couldn't think of anything else I fell back on the family".

An unpublished 1945 cartoon from the artist's collection shows Giles holding his drawing pad sitting near a destroyed house in war-torn Germany. Nearby, sitting on a pile of rubble is a Tommie who is saying to Giles "Musso gorn, Goering gorn – you'll be in the cart when they've all gorn – won't 'ave nuffin to draw, will you?"

The creation of the Giles family enabled the cartoonist to get over his initial concerns and Giles found, to our great advantage, in the intricacies of our national life, a plentiful further source of humour for almost 40 more years. The family became a stable ingredient in his work, and the canvas on which to paint the unfolding story of a country's mores and society. The family appeared in around one-sixth of his total collection of cartoons.

Giles' main characters are the four adults, Father, Mother, Grandma and Vera, with her silent presence in the family, along with eldest son George and the children operating a divisive, but highly effective, rebel group within the general family fabric. The family pets are headed up by Butch based on the real-life Butch in the Giles household (see opposite).

The family tree on the back cover, which is Giles's attempt to make some sense of his creation, also includes Rush the family spaniel. Rush appeared in the very early family cartoons while in the vast majority of cartoons, Butch the Airedale was the family pet. Over the years there were several living Butches.

There are some minor members of the family, such as Stinker, an elusive child with a mop of black hair – present at family gatherings and frequently up to no good. It appears he has taken on the role of capturing on camera some of the family's antics and often he has brought along his equipment to record events. The likely explanation for his presence is he is a neighbour's child who finds the Giles family as intriguing as we do and manages to be present when interesting things are happening.

With the ups and downs of today's life we can perhaps share, through the various Giles family members and their antics, a perspective of a society which is not so dissimilar from our own. This perhaps goes some way to explaining the resurgence in the warmth towards, and popularity of, all things Giles.

John Field

Grandma

O.K., lady – your Anglo-American Study Group went home hours ago."

Daily Express, July 20, 1954

An accident in South Carolina involving a US military aircraft carrying nuclear weapons, caused some debate. US and UK aircraft on special operational and training exercises, carried such weapons over Britain.

"Honey, will you kindly explain to you Mama that not every top-sergeant at the Base is radioactive."

Daily Express, March 22, 1958

"That was a bright stroke telling Grandma there is a famous Grandma-artist in America who is 100 years old and didn't take up painting till she was 77."

Daily Express, September 6, 1960

"We don't think Madam is remotely interested in purchasing a £15,000 yacht – we think Madam has just looked in to thaw her tootsies."

Daily Express, January 2, 1962

"They're not going to like it at home – spending the week's grocery money on Scotch."

Sunday Express, January 19, 1964

"I dare any one of you."

Daily Express, June 29, 1967

"I don't know why she's 'ollering. She's never sent a letter with a stamp on yet."

Sunday Express, September 15, 1968

"You can take that down. Thanks to Clay and Frazier, Vicar's talk on the love life of the Laughing Kookaburra Bird had a very poor attendance last Tuesday."

Daily Express, March 16, 1971

"It all started when he swopped 'Watchdog' for 'interfering old lady dog.'"

Daily Express, October 3, 1972

The newspapers had reported that a pilot on a BOAC flight, with 125 passengers aboard, began nodding off; he roused himself to find that his two co-pilots and the flight engineer were all sound asleep.

"I don't think our Captain will doze off – I've just slipped a couple of my Laxitivo Pills in his tea."

Daily Express, December 14, 1972

"Fifteen rounds for who's having my last pound of rump."

Daily Express, May 25, 1979

On July 29, 1981 Prince Charles married Lady Diana Spencer

"Your invitation's come, Mam. Please let 'em know if you wish to go by glass wedding coach or open landau."

Daily Express, May 28, 1981

"I took one to bits to prove it was all British, but she found the hands were made in Taiwan"

Daily Express, February 17, 1983

"That one doesn't need to dress up for Halloween."

Daily Express, October 31, 1985

"The lady says she's going to be a grandma and would you like a Downing Street job as an Advisory Executive?"

Sunday Express, September 4, 1988

"Mum! Grandma's gone down behind the piano."

Daily Express, December 28, 1974

"We've got to sign an agreement that in the event of a future water shortage no way will they have to share a bath with Grandma"

Daily Express, January 23, 1983

Father

"I should have thought we could have managed without your contribution to Mother's Day."

Sunday Express, March 19, 1950

"Dad's getting on well with the neighbours, Mum."

Daily Express, September 7, 1951

"Why – if it isn't that dear little man who wanted to see us home after the dance last night."

Daily Express, June 3, 1952

"Now for peace sake – don't tell the Missus we've had a drink."

Sunday Express, December 27, 1953

"This delegation wishes to register a strong protest about Father Christmases who come home late and forget to fill our socks."

Sunday Express, December 25, 1955

"Anybody seen one that matches this one? Escaped half an hour ago."

Daily Express, August 2, 1958

"Here comes Father. Best case of 'Time-will-not-change-thee' I've ever met."

Daily Express, May 18, 1959

"It's real water, Dad. Grandma's blowing bubbles."

Daily Express, January 6, 1961

"And WHY can't I sit here looking like this with the Government spending more than any other country in promoting Britain as a tourist attraction?"

Daily Express, March 16, 1961

"Davidson sends down a Chinaman – Subba Row plays it to silly mid-off, through the covers to the boundary for four, but the umpire has signalled 'No ball', etc..."

Sunday Express, July 9, 1961

Most football matches that weekend were cancelled due to bad weather.

"I told him as there's no football he can stay at home and amuse the children."

Sunday Express, January 20, 1963

A Government report had revealed the extent to which some landlords went to in order to bully their tenants into leaving their homes, such as spilling itching powder on bedding.

"Those tenants who've only got snakes in their bathroom are lucky"

Sunday Express, March 14, 1965

In the summer of '66 the country was on the brink of an economic crisis.

"Now say Sorry to Teddy for knocking him off the table - it's not his fault we've got another crisis."

Daily Express, July 21, 1966

"Hi, George! We've just popped in for a quick one with your wife before Christmas - like you asked us at the party last night".

Daily Express, December 22, 1966

"Here we are George – tickets for Silverstone. Pick you all up 2 a.m. Saturday morning."

Daily Express, April 27, 1967

"Come on, boyso,' he said, 'let's see if we can make a Henry Cooper out of you'."

Daily Express, December 3, 1970

"Surely it's not too much to ask you to amuse them for a few minutes before you go to work – I've got them all day"

Daily Express, July 22, 1971

"What do you mean – they say they needn't go back till next Wednesday?"

Daily Express, December 27, 1973

Although the post-war food rationing had finally finished two decades before, Britain was still suffering from intermittent periods of shortages.

"Ask him why, if he won the Battle of Britain, are we still short of sugar?"

Sunday Express, September 15, 1974

"'George', I said, 'Christmas Eve. What better time to ask our new neighbours round for a drink and meet Mummy'."

Daily Express, December 24, 1974

"Funny, it looked much bigger at the Boat Show."

Sunday Express, January 12, 1975

"I suppose your mother financed you for this Father's Day joke."

Sunday Express, June 19, 1977

"Which show did you say Bridget's new boy friend would have been on but for the TV strike – Eurovision or the Muppets?"

Sunday Express, March 11, 1979

"Just two more days of the Year of the Child then the Year of the Adult takes over in this house."

Sunday Express, December 30, 1979

It had been reported that, allegedly, a national newspaper had paid a woman £250,000 for her story relating to Peter Sutcliffe, known as the "Yorkshire Ripper".

"Fleet Street will give a bomb for this tape of what dad said when Aunt Florrie phoned to say they were all coming to tea."

Sunday Express, May 10, 1981

Mrs Thatcher had just promised drastic cuts for the country.

"I hope the Prime Minister makes a better job of her carving than your father."

Sunday Express, June 12, 1983

"All these long sunny walks dad's taking us on – we'll get ever so brown."

"I AM NOT SHOUTING! I'm simply stating you're not taking me out for a Father's Day lunch in this!"

Sunday Express, June 15, 1986

In 1988 MPs backed a six-month experiment to allow cameras in the Commons Chamber.

"Right, I've just sold the TV set!"

Daily Express, February 9, 1988

"Come and say 'Good Morning' to what you called 'The sweetest Christmas present you have had.'"

Daily Express, December 27, 1956

Mother

A replica of the Mayflower (Mayflower II) was completed in April 1957. It set sail from Brixham on the April 20, and arrived in Plymouth June 13.

"Why's Dad trying to book a single reservation on the Mayflower?"

Sunday Express, April 14, 1957

That Scoutmaster said something when he said Scouts deserve a well-earned rest after their strenuous bob-a-job week.

Sunday Express, April 13, 1958

Mother's Day. Give her a rest from cooking – take her out for a picnic.

Sunday Express, March 27, 1960

Cassius Clay's fight with Sonny Liston in February 1964 was broadcast at 3am GMT.

"Prize fights from Telstar at six in the morning is early enough – all transistor radios, if you please."

Daily Express, February 25, 1964

"Never mind what they said in Parliament yesterday about the arts being a vital element in our whole standard of living, my lady."

Daily Express, April 29, 1965

The Country was held in suspense for several weeks before the Prime minister announced, two days after this cartoon appeared, that a General Election would be held on March 31.

"It's too bad of Mr. Wilson to keep us all in this state of nervous tension about the election date."

Sunday Express, February 27, 1966

"Come in, Robbie Burns – we've only been waiting an hour and a half to sing Auld Lang Syne."

Sunday Express, January 1, 1967

"Mum, can our Arms to South Africa debating group use the front room on Christmas Eve?"

Daily Express, December 19, 1967

"Instant flu-cure coming up – tell your father wee Jock wants to know if he can come out for a New Year drink."

Sunday Express, December 31, 1967

"In view of his team being knocked out of the Cup yesterday, for goodness sake let him win."

Sunday Express, January 3, 1971

"Me, jealous? No! They practically live in the kitchen since I engaged an au pair girl to help."

Daily Express, December 30, 1971

"Softening up His Lordship as his team was clobbered yesterday before we remind him Auntie Milly has arrived for the week."

Sunday Express, August 13, 1972

It had been announced that home and business telephone bills would be subject to a 10% tax on the rental, plus 10% on all calls.

"The house is on fire and I've broken my leg apprehending a burglar – ask your dad if it's all right for me to dial 999."

Daily Express, March 29, 1973

The day before, Olga Korbut, winner of three Gold Olympic medals arrived in Britain with other members of the Russian gymnastic team for a three-day display at Earl's Court.

"Thank little Olga for taking their minds off football."

Sunday Express, May 6, 1973

"As a matter of fact we do not think this is better than taking one of those chancy holidays in the Med."

Sunday Express, July 28, 1974

"In the fever and excitement of yesterday's F.A. quarter finals, I hope you all remembered the Mother's Day flowers."

Sunday Express, March 9, 1975

"They're voting what to call Grandma after the Sex Discrimination Act begins tomorrow – 'Jaws' or Sir'"

Sunday Express, December 28, 1975

"I don't know who it is – we thought it was you."

Daily Express, December 24, 1976

"When I said build them a tree-house to keep them quiet, I didn't mean to include room service."

Sunday Express, July 24, 1977

"Grandma! That's enough Ooh! Cor! Wow! and Well I never! We'd ALL like to have a look at the new Daily Star."

Daily Express, November 2, 1978

"You'll spoil their Mother's Day if you're going to sit there muttering: 'They charged them £6.50 for that?'"

Sunday Express, March 25, 1979

The Iranian embassy was stormed by SAS commandos on May 5, 1980.

"Message from H.Q.: 'All S.A.S. men will enter by the back door,'"

Daily Express, May 8, 1980

"Awake my love, 'tis Father's Day – for a special treat you've got football all the afternoon on TV."

Sunday Express, June 20, 1982

At the Old Bailey, a jury was given a 24-hour police protection.

"There are enough sitting down for meals in this house without your four jury bodyguards"

Daily Express, September 14, 1982

"Remember last night? 1983 is going to be different – we're all going to live like they do in The Good Life on TV."

Daily Express, January 4, 1983

"Of course Daddy will be upset to learn Boy George has changed his hairstyle – but don't tell him now."

Daily Express, September 2, 1984

"Noel! I've just won a Christmas holiday for one in the Bahamas – plane leaves tonight!"

Daily Express, December 20, 1984

"We sure got sex-equality in this house – he's switched the washing machine on and lifted the ironing board from the cupboard all on his own."

Daily Express, November 17, 1987

Vera

"If things like this keep happening to Vera I'm afraid she's going to develop a dreadful un-American complex."

Daily Express, June 30, 1948

"If it wasn't for people like Vera we wouldn't want a health service."

Daily Express, March 29, 1952

"We're all right now – they've sold Vera six gross of post cards of the town hall in case they're out of print after Wednesday."

Daily Express, July 7, 1959

"Stop fretting, Vera – powerboats have to give way to sail."

Daily Express, September 6, 1962

In December 1963 questions were raised in the House of Commons as to why 350 baby grey seals were culled on the Farne Islands.

"Our Vera thought she heard a baby seal calling for help."

Daily Express, December 7, 1963

"Off come the health charges – back come all Vera's aches and snuffles."

Daily Express, November 5, 1964

In a newsletter interview, heart transplant pioneer Dr. Barnard had replied to critics regarding transplant operations.

"Watch 'im Vera – he'll have your heart out and shove it in Mrs. Harris before you can say Happy New Year."

Daily Express, January 4, 1968

"If we don't smoke or eat we'll all grow up healthy and happy like Auntie Vera"

Daily Express, April 3, 1969

"Grandma, you must let Vera vote for whom she chooses."

Daily Express, June 18, 1970

"Here's a story to warm the cockles of your heart, Vera – it will take at least two million years to erode the astronauts' footprints on the moon."

Daily Express, May 16, 1977

"You realise her snuffle and your phoney knee have taken a bigger cut of that £8,000 million than all the mod-rocks and football punch-ups put together?"

Daily Express, October 10, 1978

The BBC had revealed plans to axe 1,500 jobs over a two-year period to save the sum.

"Vera thinks she's helping the BBC save its £130 million by not switching it on."

Sunday Express, March 2, 1980

"Ah! The good news, Vera – Thatcher's invited Reagan to build a germ warfare station half a mile up the road"

Daily Express, March 12, 1981

The Dogs Trust had introduced the slogan 'A dog is for life not just for Christmas'

"Vera read about all those little dogs that wanted a home after Christmas."

Sunday Express, December 30, 1984

Children

"It says here that when your teacher explained that the Nations of the World were striving in unity towards a glorious Peace, you emitted a long, low rumbling noise resembling the sound 'Burrrrrrrp'."

Daily Express, July 24, 1947

"I want to go home."

Daily Express, June 12, 1948

"Mum! That man's thrown all our toffee and oranges out of the window."

Daily Express, July 31, 1951

"Caravan? The caravan came off hours ago."

Daily Express, September 11, 1951

"And now, if the last boy to leave school on November 5 will kindly step forward..."

Daily Express, November 6, 1951

"It has been reported that you left your post yesterday afternoon without permission and went to the Motor Show."

Daily Express, October 23, 1952

"Look out, Dad! Here comes the man to say no more Highland Games rehearsals."

Sunday Express, September 5, 1954

"Not only are these milk tablets issued to schools highly beneficial, but most children prefer them."

Daily Express, March 8, 1955

"Cancel Children's Hour for Wimbledon, would they? We can soon fix that."

Sunday Express, July 3, 1955

National Safety Campaign No. 1

Daily Express, May 31, 1956

National Safety Campaign No. 2.

Daily Express, June 2, 1956

National Safety Campaign No. 3.

Daily Express, June 6, 1956

The possibility of banning boxing was being discussed by some people and, in that year, Fidel Castro introduced a ban on professional boxing in Cuba.

"I hope I grow tall enough to clip Chalky one across the ear just once before they ban boxing."

Sunday Express, June 7, 1959

The Royal Commission on the Police reports that there is insufficient readiness on the part of the public to help the Police.

Sunday Express, June 3, 1962

The Electricians' Trade Union had instructed its members to ban overtime, leading to power failures.

"It wasn't the power cut – I just switched the light off"

Daily Express, January 15, 1963

"Dad! There's nearly six inches of it in the drive again."

Sunday Express, February 3, 1963

The day before, the coupling of US spacecraft Gemini 9 with a satellite had been unsuccessful.

"Dad – I think a piece of Gemini 9 is just going to land on Mr. Jones's greenhouse."

Sunday Express, June 5, 1966

"It would have to be a handy-sized aircraft to make enough noise to get through to this house."

Daily Express, July 28, 1966

A new televised version of Alice in Wonderland had been deemed unsuitable for children.

"The old folks are at home watching Alice in Wonderland."

Sunday Express, November 27, 1966

There had been a recent case of an "aeroplane being worried" by a kite flying over Regent's Park.

"Sorry to disturb you, Sir, but the Air Ministry inform us that thanks to your boy's .... kite all London Airport planes have been diverted to Gatwick and Manchester"

Sunday Express, May 3, 1970

Three days earlier, Tony Jacklin had won the US Open Golf Championship.

"Thank Tony Jacklin for the course crawling with golf-mad truants."

Daily Express, June 25, 1970

"She'll give you 'Sportsman of the Year' if you miss."

Daily Express, November 14, 1972

"Putting children up for adoption on TV has started something."

Daily Express, May 14, 1974

"You'll have to find somewhere safer than the top of the cupboard to hide the presents – they've found Dad's."

Sunday Express, December 12, 1976

"We'd like separate bills and 5% off for cash."

Sunday Express, July 23, 1978

"Finish making Grandma's Easter egg later and tell her breakfast is ready."

Sunday Express, April 6, 1980

"Miss Potter in History taught us all they did was land over here and build good roads"

Daily Express, October 21, 1980

"Mum, how many Centenary Telegrams has Grandma had from the Queen?"

Sunday Express, October 3, 1982

"Those Teddy bears you 'found' up here and put in Christie's sale were the twins' Christmas presents."

Sunday Express, December 15, 1985

OAPs had just been given an increase in their fuel allowance.

"Grandma's making sure she gets her extra £5 worth."

Sunday Express, January 18, 1987

Pets

"Bridget read that cats should be kept indoors because cats don't like fireworks."

Daily Express, November 4, 1950

"Stand by for some lengthy reminiscing on 'Now-when-I-was-in Manchester...'"

Daily Express, June 12, 1951

"The man in the pet shop told Vera that all his little birds would starve after Budget Day unless somebody bought them."

Daily Express, March 7, 1952

"I can't think of anything this family wanted more than to win a pony."

Daily Express, May 5, 1955

"I'd show him who's favourite in this house if they ever let him out for a fly round the room."

Daily Express, September 15, 1957

There had been reports of a woman who could 'talk' mice and rats out of a house.

"Mother – remember you asked our mice to leave and they all moved in next door?"

Daily Express, February 15, 1962

The authorities had just produced a leaflet on birth control featuring Casanova courting a young woman.

"Pity you can't train that damn dog of yours to read a few Casanova posters."

Daily Express, December 31, 1970

Two days earlier the Prime Minister, Edward Heath, had been given the go-ahead by the Commons to sign the treaty providing for Britain's accession to the European Community.

"Dad – a gentleman's called to say Butch has just made his contribution to the Common Market"

Sunday Express, January 23, 1972

Due to a dock strike, farmers were considering asking the Government to use emergency powers to protect animal feed supplies.

"In view of the animal feeding stuffs crisis do you think we might persuade you-know-who to supplement his rations by catching the odd mouse."

Daily Express, August 8, 1972

"This lady claims that your dog has just devalued her Crufts champ."

Sunday Express, February 11, 1973

"O.K. Grandma, I've found the little top ones you dropped – Butch has got 'em in his basket."

Daily Express, January 17, 1974

"Everyone else in the road have had their polling cards, Butch. I repeat – everyone else in the road have had their poling cards, Butch..."

Daily Express, February 26, 1974

"As we haven't had beef for so long I thought I'd be rash and treat ourselves to a piece of sirloin."

Sunday Express, May 12, 1974

"That leaves you Butch or Grandma."

Sunday Express, August 10, 1975

"Butch's breakfast menu: two cotton reels, Grandma's slippers, 1oz. Dad's tobacco, one Daily Express, half-shovel coal, half-hundredweight Bonio – yes, I suppose you could say pets eat more than children."

Daily Express, September 23, 1975

"It's all right Dad – Bill's hamster has reversed the charge for his call to Butch."

Daily Express, October 2, 1975

"Shut up, Butch, wait till we see what he does tomorrow."

Daily Express, April 10, 1978

"Right – on the show of hands Sebastian gets a reprieve – one of you go to the shop and get six large tins of corned beef."

Sunday Express, December 17, 1978

"You've bought Grandma a WHAT for Christmas?"

Sunday Express, December 21, 1980

"They've read about that Post Office cat who scared off those raiders."

Daily Express, February 5, 1981

"How do you keep fireworks away from a pet who's just eaten all your Atomic Bangers?"

Daily Express, November 5, 1981

"Dad, you know the Consumers Association said a goose is a better guard dog than a dog?"

Daily Express, November 24, 1981

There had been a report that a dog answered the phone when its owner was out.

"Don't disturb Butch – he's calling that little Jack Russell who answers telephones"

Daily Express, March 10, 1983

"Moral obligations being all the rage – I suggest you teach that Airedale thing of yours a few."

"Butch must learn that the law that says it's all right for pretty nude dancers to bite policemen, doesn't apply to grumpy Airedales."

Sunday Express, November 6, 1983

"Mind you don't make them too fat to fly away from the cat!"

Sunday Express, January 20, 1985

"Butch would have won – but I think he dropped a few points when he took the sleeve out of the judge's jacket."

Sunday Express, February 10, 1985

"He's never nipped anyone before – he probably thought you were going to mug him."

Daily Express, December 24, 1985

"You're wasting your time, cat – the most she'll leave you is her lucky charm and half a bottle of peppermints."

Daily Express, May 12, 1988

"We rescued him from the London Zoo."

Daily Express, October 15, 1989

"Just because our Butch had your Teddy Bear's ear hardly puts him in the pit bull terrier class."

Sunday Express, May 26, 1991

Cartoons

British Cartoon Archive

Carl Giles

All the cartoons in this book were copied from material in Carl Giles' own private archive, which is held by the British Cartoon Archive at the University of Kent.

The Giles archive was donated to the British Cartoon Archive in 2005, and contains a vast amount of material. It begins in 1942, the year before Giles joined the Sunday Express, because all his cartoons and papers from before that date were destroyed in the London Blitz. From that point onwards he kept almost everything, either at his farm at Witnesham or his studio in nearby Ipswich, and his private archive grew to include almost 6,000 original cartoon drawings and 1,500 cartoon prints, plus a vast image library of cuttings and photographs, correspondence, reference books, and studio paraphernalia.

As his artwork piled up, Giles wondered what to do with it. He joked that "I'll probably flog the lot!", but he only ever gave away his cartoon drawings to friends, or donated them to charity auctions. By his seventieth birthday he had so many drawings bundled up in his barn at Witnesham that he needed a strategy. "We could have a little fire one day," he said half-jokingly to one interviewer, "and solve the whole problem." But on his death in 1995 he in fact left his entire archive to a special Carl Giles Cartoon Trust, which donated it to the British Cartoon Archive ten years later.

The British Cartoon Archive has since catalogued the entire Giles archive, and made it freely available through its website at www.cartoons.ac.uk Fans of Giles can now view nearly 8,500 of his cartoons from 1937 to 1993, plus almost 800 documents and photographs, from his wartime identity card - in his real name of Ronald Giles, which he hated - to pictures of his beloved yachts.

The British Cartoon Archive holds the national collection of political and social-comment cartoons from British newspapers and magazines. It has over 120,000 original drawings, and its catalogue at www.cartoons. ac.uk includes almost 160,000 cartoons, dating from 1790 to the present day.

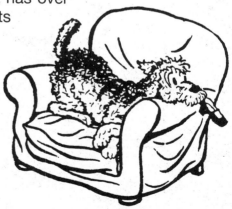

Butch, Giles's Dog